Table of Conten

Stitch patterns

Projects

Straight-Line Quilting Overview

In straight-line machine quilting, the stitch length and direction of stitches are determined by the machine. A "walking foot" replaces the standard presser foot to ensure that the three quilt layers move through the machine as a single unit.

Quilting a straight line requires a slower speed than the speed you sewed the quilt-top pieces. A medium speed gives the walking foot and the bottom feed dogs ample opportunity to grab and move the quilt sandwich.

No sewing machine is engineered to pull your quilt up off the floor, over the tabletop and into the machine. Guiding the quilt sandwich is your responsibility. Make sure there are no obstructions in the way.

Plan the order you will sew your lines in advance. You can start in the center and work out to the sides, or you can begin on one side and finish at the other. The choice is often dictated by the pattern. Sewing from the center out is often the best option.

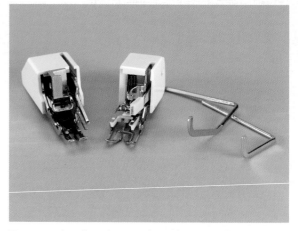

Two typical walking feet. To the right are guide bars that fit in the walking foot or presser-foot holder.

Prepare the Machine

Follow these steps to prepare your machine for straight-line quilting.

1 Attach the walking foot.

2 Make sure the stitch is set for straight-line sewing with the needle in the center position.

3 If one is available for your machine, insert the single-needle plate.

4 Set the stitch length for 2.5. This is often the default setting for computerized machines. It is a standard medium-length stitch.

5 Thread the machine.

Rest elbows comfortably at the sides, place hands on either side of the needle, slightly in front of it. When ready to reposition the hands, stop the machine, move the hands, then resume sewing. Straight lines become crooked lines when the hands are removed while the needle is still moving.

Free-Motion Quilting Oveview

In free-motion machine quilting, the stitch length and direction of stitches are determined by the quilter. The three quilt layers move through the machine in all directions as a single unit completely under your control. To help the machine create smooth stitches, you attach a darning foot or a free-motion foot.

There are generally two postures for free-motion machine quilting. They both have to do with how you prefer to move the quilt sandwich. See photos at right. Notice that the hands are placed on both sides of the needle.

Note: I always quilt using some type of gripping gloves. However, for the purpose of demonstration, gloves were not used.

In the second position, the elbows rest on the edge of the table surface or the extension table. The quilt layers are moved by the fingertips and wrists, ideal for smaller free-motion stitch patterns.

Prepare the Machine

Follow these steps to prepare your machine for free-motion quilting.

1 Attach the free-motion foot or darning foot.

2 Lower the feed dogs. It is not necessary to set the stitch length. Once the feed dogs are lowered, the stitch length is determined by the quilter.

3 Make sure the stitch is set for straight-line sewing with the needle in the center position.

4 If one is available for your machine, insert the single-needle plate.

5 Thread the machine.

Poor hand position results in poor stitches and pattern formation.

Hint

The feed dogs in some machines do not lower. Instead, a square plate is attached to cover the feed dogs. These covers are often cumbersome. If your machine has a cover, consider using the Free-Motion Slider. It is not bothered by the feed dogs and will enable you to move your quilt sandwich freely.

Straight-Line Quilting

Benefits

Requires no marking.

Very fast for place mats and other small projects.

For large quilts, it helps stabilize the layers until the remainder of the quilting is completed.

Emphasizes the difference between sections or fabrics.

Drawbacks

Adds minimal texture to the quilt top.

It can be difficult to get the needle into the "ditch."

For intricately pieced blocks, stitch in the ditch requires rotating the quilt many times.

Stitch in the Ditch

Stitch in the ditch is simply stitching directly into the seams of the quilt. By adding depth at the seam, this technique emphasizes the break from one fabric to the next. The viewer's eye is drawn to fabric prints, unusual piecing or appliqué techniques rather than to the actual quilting.

Stitch in the ditch is accomplished by aligning the needle to the seams and sewing right into the seams. The stitches lay flat on the bottom fabric of the seam. Any thread can be used for stitch in the ditch.

Stitch in the ditch is a strong, durable application, but with so many quilting options, you don't want to limit yourself to this technique.

In this example, stitch in the ditch emphasizes the "fussy-cut" novelty squares. Quilted diagonal lines push the green and pink fabric to the background.

Stitch in the ditch was relatively easy to use for this 6" (15cm) block. However, it required stopping to rotate the layers eighteen times. Imagine doing that to many stars in a large project.

In this holiday example, metallic thread was used.

Parallel Diagonal Lines

To quilt parallel diagonal lines you will need a 24" × 6" (61cm × 15cm) rotary cutting ruler and a marker. Place the 45° line of the ruler directly over one of the side seams connecting the border and quilt center. Larger quilts will require that you use more than one ruler; butt them together end to end to complete your marks.

Line up the 45° line to the side seam that attaches the quilt center to the border.

Hint

Be sure to place the 45° line of the ruler on the seam that connects the border and quilt top. This seam is much straighter than the outer raw edge of the border fabric.

Parallel diagonal lines stitched 2" (5cm) apart. Because the quilting is not dense, I topstitched the decorative border to the top and eliminated the need for binding—a treatment less suitable with dense quilting.

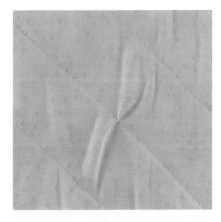

Avoid stitching a fold into the backing by pin basting carefully and by guiding the layers evenly into the machine with both hands.

Benefits

Simplest straight-line quilting pattern.

Easy to mark. You can use the quilting guide bar in place of marking each individual line.

Makes a quick and easy border treatment.

Fast for place mats and other small projects.

Drawbacks

Adds minimal texture to the quilt top.

Possible to stitch a fold in the backing fabric if you stretch the quilt sandwich diagonally while feeding the layers into the machine.

Diagonal Squares

Forty-five-degree diagonal squares are formed by marking two sets of parallel diagonal lines. In all of the samples here, the lines were marked 2" (5cm) apart.

The first set of markings uses one of the 45° lines of the ruler lined up on the seam that joins the border to the quilt. When marking, complete all the diagonal lines in the first direction at the same time.

Benefits

Easy to sew.

Results are predictable and geometric.

Relatively quick if the rows are not too close together.

Nondirectional (no matter which side you view the quilt, the pattern remains the same).

Drawbacks

All lines need to be marked for accurate results on a large project.

Possible to stitch a fold in the backing fabric if you stretch the quilt sandwich diagonally while feeding the layers into the machine.

The second set of marks comes from rotating the ruler so that the other 45° line on the ruler is aligned with the same side seam. Complete the marks going in the opposite direction.

First diagonal direction

Second diagonal direction

Hint

The distance between lines determines how dense the overall quilting will be. Two inches (5cm) yields good coverage and meets batting requirements for stitching density. You may sew lines closer together for the background of an appliqué project or for a border area.

Diamonds

Diamonds are formed by completing two sets of marked lines using your ruler's 30° lines. Place one of the 30° lines directly over one of the side seams connecting the border and quilt top. In all the samples here, the lines were marked 1½" (3.8cm) apart, yielding good coverage and meeting batting requirements for stitching density.

The first set of markings uses one of the 30° lines of the ruler lined up on a side seam that joins the border to the quilt. Mark all the diagonal lines in that direction.

  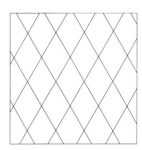

The second set of marks comes from rotating the ruler so that the opposite 30° line is aligned with the same side seam. Complete the marks going in the opposite direction.

Marking Pattern

Benefits

Easy to sew.

More interesting than the 45° diagonal lines.

Drawbacks

Must be marked.

Directional (only looks good in one direction).

30° lines of the ruler can be confusing at first.

Additional Designs

Stitch the diagonal lines as marked, then sew horizontal lines to create equilateral triangles. The horizontal lines do not need to be marked.

The diagonal lines do not have to line up to the angles of a pieced block. They can be sewn on any quilt surface, and they will always look elegant.

Sew a set of diamonds in one color, then sew the echo lines in another color. If you use the guide bar for the echo lines, you will only have to mark one set of lines.

Squares

Squares are formed by marking sets of vertical and horizontal lines that are parallel to the top and side seams of the border. In the example, the lines were marked 2" (5cm) apart. This does not produce a very interesting quilt, but it is a great starting point for many other more interesting patterns.

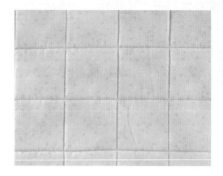

Additional Designs

Add diagonal lines in both directions. It's a great look that is simple to sew, and you don't have to mark the diagonal lines.

Adding diagonal lines in only one direction results in an interesting dissonant look.

Add one vertical echo line and two horizontal echo lines to make rectangles, a great look for place mats.

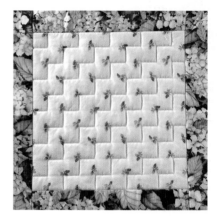

Horizontal and vertical lines marked 1" (2.5cm) apart with quilting that looks like steps or a diagonal zigzag line.

This quilted star has densely quilted horizontal and vertical lines that never intersect. They force the eye to the center of the star.

Benefits

Easy to sew.

Results are predictable.

Quick (if the rows of stitching are not too close together).

Nondirectional.

Drawbacks

Lines need to be marked for accurate results on a large project.

Echo Quilting

Echo quilting occurs when a line is sewn parallel to a quilting line, a seam line or a fabric motif.

Special Designs

As long as you are willing to mark, sew and rotate, any straight-line design can be quilted with a walking foot. Keep in mind rotating the quilt requires stopping with the needle down, lifting the presser foot, rotating the quilt, putting the presser foot back down and continuing to sew to the next turn.

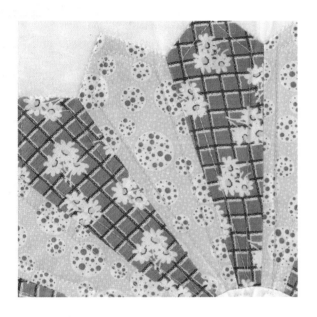

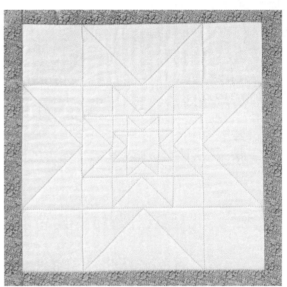

Benefits

Requires no marking.

Predictable results.

Nondirectional.

Drawbacks

Requires rotating the quilt.

Cumbersome to do for a large quilt.

> **Hint**
>
> By echo quilting, you can create additional designs while only marking one grid, especially if you use a guide bar.

Benefits

Beautiful to look at.

Interesting and recognizable.

Drawbacks

Almost always requires that the quilt sandwich be rotated many times.

Requires advanced planning and marking.

Cumbersome to do for a large project.

Unmarked Free-Motion Quilting

Stitch in the Ditch

Many novice quilters believe stitch in the ditch is strictly a straight-line quilting technique, but it is often used to quilt around an appliqué design to provide stability to the quilt layers without adding visible stitches around the appliqué.

Stitch in the ditch is accomplished by sewing right into the seams.

I stitched the umbrella and duckie all the way around to meet batting requirements. The raindrop fabric looked beautiful without quilting lines, so no other quilting was desirable.

Benefits

Requires no marking.

Helps to puff out an appliqué design.

Drawbacks

Adds minimal texture.

Difficult to get the needle into the "ditch."

Random Meandering

Random meandering is one of the most versatile stitch patterns for free-motion quilting enthusiasts. It adds texture without distraction, and it can be sewn in any size.

Hint

When random meandering, novice quilters tend to speed up the pace the quilt layers are moved over the sewing bed. But they fail to speed up the rate of the machine, creating very large or inconsistent stitches, especially when the pattern is large. Be sure you keep a steady rhythm.

Benefits

Easy to sew.

Used in a background, it forces the background to the back.

Adds texture without taking center stage.

Versatile and graceful.

Nondirectional.

Drawbacks

Is used quite often.

Difficult to maintain consistent stitches.

Loops

Loops create a whimsical look on a textured quilt surface. They are formed by combining graceful, wavy lines and loops.

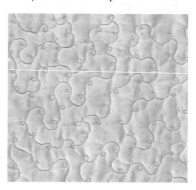

Hint

To create a random look for your loops, try alternating between clockwise and counterclockwise formations.

Benefits

Ideal in a juvenile novelty print.

Fast to quilt.

Great with variegated threads.

Good for connecting other designs, such as leaves and flowers.

Drawbacks

Difficult to use in tight spaces.

Difficult to keep random.

Flames

Flames are formed with wavy snake lines and sharp points. The technique takes a little getting used to, but with practice you'll get the hang of it.

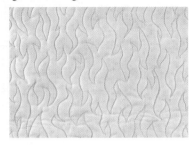

Hint

If your tension becomes poor at the top of the pattern, stop the needle at the tip of the point before you continue sewing. You only need to stop for a moment. A momentary pause at sharp points can make a big difference.

Benefits

Add excitement to the quilt surface.

Looks great with metallic thread.

Drawbacks

Highly recognizable.

Won't work with some fabric themes, such as a 1930s reproduction quilt.

Difficult to maintain consistent spacing and random appearance.

Thread tension can be poor at the tip of the flame.

If stitched vertically, flames are highly directional.

Landscape Texture

Landscape texture is formed by making long horizontal lines, small curves and short vertical lines. It has the effect of looking like water, snow or clouds. There is no diagonal movement.

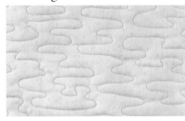

Used vertically with variegated thread, landscape texture also makes great bark texture for a tree.

Benefits

Effective in a landscape quilt.

Good for borders on a busy print.

Adds more texture than random meandering.

Drawbacks

Not suitable on solid-colored fabrics (unless you're quilting water on a landscape quilt).

Challenging to maintain a random pattern.

Swirls and Curls

This elegant pattern is formed with wavy lines, curvy lines and crescents. The crescents are used to echo the curls.

Swirls and curls stitched on a marbled fabric using variegated blue thread.

Benefits

Nondirectional.

Creates an unexpected texture when used as an allover design.

Crescent points are good for a tight corner.

Drawbacks

Not a strong geometric texture.

Thread tension can be poor at the tip of the crescent.

Unmarked Free-Motion Quilting Combinations

Teardrops

Circles and teardrops are very versatile. The example below uses teardrops as the basis for the pattern. The circles are combined with echo quilting. The echo quilting lines enable you to get from one place to the next in order to fill in the areas. It can be stitched out in all sizes.

Pachysandra

Pachysandra is formed by combining echo teardrops, flower petal leaves and echo quilting. The small flower center and the echo quilting are dense stitching lines quilted among large, puffy flower petals. The contrast between dense stitching and puffy leaves adds wonderful texture to a quilt surface.

Leaves and Flowers

Many leaves and flowers exist in nature. In quilting, there are even more, ranging from realistic to whimsical. Combine them with stems, wavy lines and loops for endless possibilities.

Hint
Teardrops and circles make a lovely inner-border treatment.

Marked Free-Motion Quilting

Tracing and Pre-Printed Panels

Pre-printed fabric panels can be quilted using any one of the previous straight-line or free-motion panels. Another option is to trace over the larger design elements of the fabric.

In this example, black thread was used on all the large flowers, butterflies and leaves. Random meandering was used in the background. The black thread and puff from the batting makes the flowers and leaves stand out more when viewed from a distance.

To enable the butterflies to stand out, they were traced with a bright colored thread.

Vines

While vines can be easily quilted without any marking lines, it may give you more confidence in the beginning to mark all or part of the design.

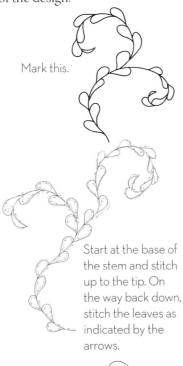

Mark this.

Start at the base of the stem and stitch up to the tip. On the way back down, stitch the leaves as indicated by the arrows.

Mark just the stems to make sure you have balanced coverage. Then start stitching in the center and travel up each stem; on the way back down, add the leaves of the vine.

Clamshells

Clamshells in any size are a beautiful quilting treatment, but they do require marking. To maintain a balanced framework, it is a good idea to draw a grid (horizontal and vertical lines) and then mark the individual clamshells with a stencil. Some clamshell stencils let you mark repeated clamshells without a grid.

In this example, the single line clamshells were marked, but echo quilting was added in two of the corners. In the opposite two corners, an additional loop was added.

Wavy Lines

Any straight-line pattern can be stitched using free-motion wavy lines. The only real challenge is to maintain your rhythm when quilting the long lines.

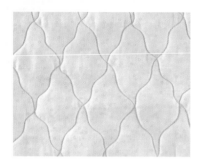

> ### Hint
>
> Another continuous line treatment is to combine free-motion straight lines with recognizable images. I like to use cookie cutters for this application. To use this technique, mark the quilt with a grid of horizontal and vertical lines so that the tracings of the cookie cutter can be spaced evenly.

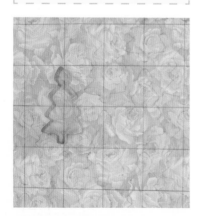

The horizontal lines will not be quilted. Only the vertical lines and the images are quilted.

Stencils

Hundreds of stencils are available today that can enhance a quilt surface. Because of the popularity of free-motion quilting, many stencils are produced in the form of continuous line designs. Some stencils come with a label that indicates the direction the design should be stitched.

Additional simple designs and new, intricate designs are available in books specifically for tracing onto paper. After the design has been traced onto the paper, it is pinned to the quilt surface. The quilter sews over the paper, tracing the designs. The tracing paper is then torn away. Any theme fabric has a counterpart somewhere in a stencil.

Another option is to trace a favorite design onto lightweight interfacing. Trace and cut many designs. Then spray the back with a temporary fabric adhesive. Place the cutouts in a uniform or random arrangement onto the quilt surface. Quilt around each image. Random meandering or stippling can be filled in between each image.

This is marked free-motion design using a heart-shaped cookie cutter as a stencil.

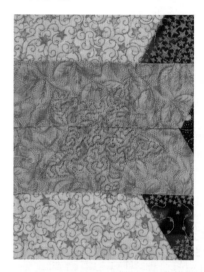

I made the stars on this quilt by quilting around star-shaped, lightweight-interfacing stencils. I then removed the stencils and stippled the inside of each star.

Quilting Individual Blocks

Any repeated block of a quilt, such as stars or nine-patch blocks, can be quilted one at a time as individual blocks. You can use a stencil or a single image that you can sew without markings.

Any free-motion design can be resized for any block.

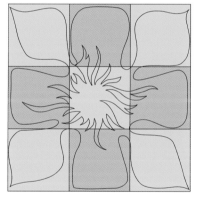

The flower here was enlarged to fill up a nine-patch block.

There are many ways to quilt individual star blocks.

The quilted star in the center of this block is formed by gluing two 1¼" (3.2cm) offset squares of paper together. Only the outline of the paper star is marked in the center of the star. The flowing lines are stitched out from the points of the center star.

Rag Quilt

This project is designed with one goal in mind: Each of the finished 8" (20.5cm) squares are quilted *before* they are pieced together. Because of this unusual construction technique, these squares are easy to use for practicing free-motion quilting, and after sewing over one-hundred squares, you will be proficient and confident using your machine for free-motion quilting. The squares start off in their raw form as 9" (23cm) squares, but you only need to fill a 7" (18cm) square area with quilting. A 9" (23cm) square is a manageable block for any quilter.

RAG QUILT Yardage Chart

Finished Size of Quilt	Total number of squares in completed project	Total number of half yard cuts of colored flannel fabrics for scrappy look	Cutting the outside flannel squares	Amount of white flannel for batting
Lap Quilt 56" × 80"	7 squares across 10 squares down 70 total squares	eighteen ½-yard cuts totaling 9 yards	Cut each ½-yard length of fabric into four pairs of 9" squares. Cut 70 pairs of 9" squares.	3¼ yards—cut fourteen 8" strips. From each strip, cut five 8" squares.
Twin Quilt 72" × 104"	9 squares across 13 squares down 117 total squares	thirty ½-yard cuts totaling 15 yards	Cut each ½-yard length of fabric into four pairs of 9" squares. Cut 117 pairs of 9" squares.	5⅔ yards—cut twenty-four 8" strips. From each strip, cut five 8" squares.
Full Quilt 88" × 112"	11 squares across 14 squares down 154 total squares	thirty-nine ½-yard cuts totaling 19½ yards	Cut each ½-yard length of fabric into four pairs of 9" squares. Cut 154 pairs of 9" squares.	7⅔ yards—cut thirty-one 8" strips. From each strip, cut five 8" squares.
Queen Quilt 96" × 112"	12 squares across 14 squares down 168 total squares	forty-two ½-yard cuts totaling 21 yards	Cut each ½-yard length of fabric into four pairs of 9" squares. Cut 168 pairs of 9" squares.	8⅓ yards—cut thirty-four 8" strips. From each strip, cut five 8" squares.
King Quilt 104" × 120"	13 squares across 15 squares down 195 total squares	forty-nine ½-yard cuts totaling 24½ yards	Cut each ½-yard length of fabric into four pairs of 9" squares. Cut 195 pairs of 9" squares.	10 yards—cut thirty-nine 8" strips. From each strip, cut five 8" squares.

Hint

Do not pre-wash the colored flannel. *Do* pre-wash the flannel batting. By washing the inside fabric, but not the outside fabric, you will create additional texture when the completed project is laundered.

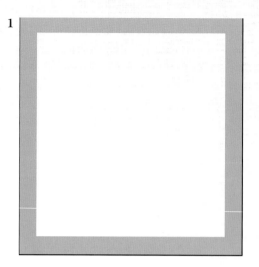

Materials

Sewing machine and tools

Neutral thread for piecing

Coordinating quilting thread

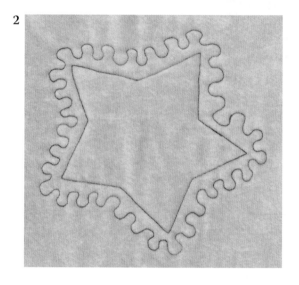

1 Sandwich one 8" (20.5cm) piece of white flannel between two 9" (23cm) squares of the print flannel. The white square is centered inside the 9" (23cm) squares as shown.

2 Quilt the 9" (23cm) flannel sandwich. Center the quilting so that there is approximately 1" (2.5cm) of unquilted space on all four sides. I used random meandering in every square of the sample with 100% cotton, solid-colored coordinating thread. However, you could quilt your project using any quilting pattern. The more variety, the more proficient in free-motion quilting you will become.

3 Repeat steps 1 and 2 until all the 9" (23cm) squares are quilted.

4 Arrange your squares using the yardage chart to determine the number of rows and columns.

5 Once the squares have been arranged, begin joining them into rows. To join squares, place them right sides together and sew using a ½" (1.3cm) seam allowance. Sew together one row at a time. You do not need to press any seams.

6 Starting at the top, join the first two rows using a ½" (1.3cm) seam allowance. As you come to intersecting seams, open each seam and continue to sew the two rows together.

7 Add each row one at a time until all the rows have been attached.

8 Once all the rows have been sewn, snip the seam allowance fabric. The snips should be made every ¼" (6mm) to ½" (1.3cm).

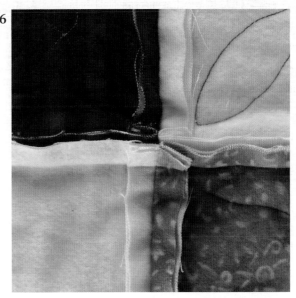

By opening the seams at each intersection where four blocks come together, you are spreading out the bulk.

Hint

Be sure not to accidentally snip the stitching at the seam. This step can be tiring, so work on a small section every day until the entire quilt is snipped.

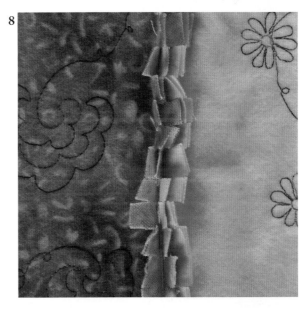

Snip the raw edges every ¼" (6mm) to ½" (1.3cm).

9 Launder the quilt. I laundered the completed sample at a commercial laundromat because of the extra large washing machines and dryers. The more wear and laundering the quilt receives, the more the edges will fray evenly for a soft, textured finish. Both sides of this quilt are the right side.

Hint

Because of the heavy nature of the flannel fabrics, it is best to use a sturdy, size 90 topstitch needle for piecing together the 9" (23cm) squares.

Americana Place Mats

Finished size: 14" × 20" (35.5cm × 51cm) before quilting

This project, comprised of four place mats, will help you do the following:

Learn to save time by planning ahead. The four place mats can be quickly pin basted one time on a single piece of backing and a single piece of batting.

Incorporate both straight-line and free-motion patterns.

Learn to balance straight-line and free-motion quilting for uniform quilt density.

Materials
(for Four Place Mats)

Sewing machine and tools

Neutral thread used for piecing

Red and navy blue thread for the appliqué

Quilting thread

6½" (16.5cm) square of fusible web for the stars of the flag

6½" × 17" (16.5cm × 43cm) piece of fusible web for the red stripes of the flag

35" × 40" (89cm × 101.5cm) piece of batting

Cutting Directions

From novelty flag fabric, cut four 13¼" × 14" (34.5cm × 35.5cm) pieces.

From the backing fabric, cut away selvage edges only. Do not cut this into four pieces.

From the white fabric, cut four 7¼" × 14" (18.5cm × 35.5cm) pieces.

From the red fabric, cut eight 1⅜" (3.5cm) strips for the single-layer binding, and 7" × 18" (18cm × 46cm) rectangle for the red flag stripes .

From the 7" (18cm) square of navy blue fabric, cut four shapes using the template on page 29. (Cut navy fabric *after* attaching paper-backed fusible web.)

Optional: Cut the napkin fabric into four equal 18" (46cm) squares.

Fabric
(for Four Place Mats)

1 yd. (91cm) or four fat quarters of a novelty flag fabric or other favorite red, white and blue fabric

1 yd. (91cm) of a novelty-print fabric for the backing

½ yd. (46cm) of white fabric for the background behind the flag

½ yd. (46cm) of red fabric for the binding and the flag stripes

7" (18cm) square of navy blue fabric with tiny white stars for the flag

Optional: 1 yd. (91cm) of coordinating fabric for square napkins (16" [40.5cm] finished size)

Hint

When cutting the novelty flag fabric, keep in mind that the 14" (35.5cm) side is sewn to the white fabric. Make sure to cut directional fabrics accordingly.

Hint

It takes a little experimentation to know how dense the free-motion quilting needs to be in comparison to the straight-line quilting. Different sewing machines will produce different results. Uniform density is important for the place mats to lay flat.

1 Trace four star sections found on page 29 onto the 6½" (16.5cm) square of fusible web for the stars of the flag. Trace twelve long red stripes and sixteen short red stripes onto the 6½" × 17" (16.5cm × 43cm) piece of fusible web for the red stripes of the flag. Stripe patterns are also found on page 29.

2 Following the manufacturer's directions, fuse the 6½" (16.5cm) square of fusible web to the wrong side of the 7" (18cm) square of navy blue fabric. Fuse the 6½" × 17" (16.5cm × 43cm) fusible web to the wrong side of the 7" × 18" (18cm × 46cm) red fabric rectangle.

3 Cut out each piece. Each place mat will use one star section, four short red stripes and three long red stripes.

4 Arrange the pieces of the flag on each of the 7¼" × 14" (18.5cm × 35.5cm) pieces of white fabric as illustrated below. After removing the paper backing, arrange the pieces of the flag on the white background.

5 Tuck the left edges of the short red stripes under the star fabric. Fuse all pieces to the background according to the directions that accompany the fusible web.

6 Thread your machine with coordinating red thread. Using a reduced-size blanket stitch or a reduced-size zigzag stitch, sew around each stripe. Do not sew the sides of the short red stripes underneath the star fabric. When the stripes are finished on all four place mats, change the thread to navy blue. Using a reduced-size blanket stitch or a reduced-size zigzag stitch, sew around each star section.

7 With right sides together, attach one white section to one novelty print section, making sure that any directional fabric is facing the same direction as the flag. Sew these 14" (35.5cm) long seams using a ¼" (6mm) seam allowance. Press the seam towards the white fabric.

8 Using a contrasting marker, mark your straight lines on the novelty print (shown below). The quilting lines of the sample are spaced 1" (2.5cm) apart.

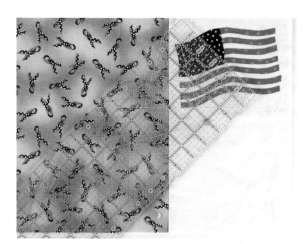

Using the 45° line on the ruler, mark your lines on the novelty print fabric in preparation for the straight-line quilting.

9 Secure the entire piece of backing fabric to your table. Smooth the batting over the backing, then evenly space each place mat top over the batting. Pin baste. When the basting is complete, separate the four place mats by cutting through the batting and backing. Then remove the masking tape.

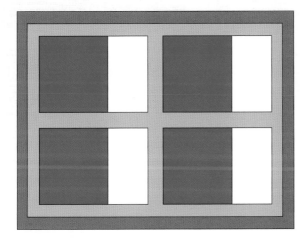

10 Straight-line quilt the novelty print area. Quilt the white section using random meandering. Stitch around the flag (shown below).

11 When the quilting is complete, cut away the excess backing and batting. Bind the place mats.

12 *Optional*: To complete the napkins, press over each raw edge to the back ¼" (6mm) around all four sides. Secure each raw edge to the back using a reduced-size zigzag stitch to eliminate fraying.

The back of the place mat shows the quilting patterns. The quilting between the red stripes makes them puff out. Stitch in the ditch was used in the seam to get from one straight line to the next in the center of the quilt.

Table Toppers

Finished size: 23" (58.5cm) diameter before quilting

The Table Toppers will help you:

> See how different quilting patterns change a quilt top.

> Use a quilting pattern that emanates from the center out.

Materials

Sewing machine and tools

Neutral thread used for piecing

Quilting thread

22½° rotary cutting ruler by Nifty Notions

7" (18cm) square of freezer paper

Two 6" (15cm) squares of
iron-on/tear-away stabilizer

40" × 48" (101.5cm × 122cm) piece of batting

Polyester monofilament thread

Fabric

Five fat quarters

8" (20.5cm) square of fabric for the
center circles

One fat quarter for the binding

1⅓ yd. (1.2m) of fabric for the backing fabric

Cutting Directions

From each of the five fat quarters,
cut six 2½" × 21" (6.5cm × 53.5cm) strips.

From the fat quarter for the binding,
cut eight 1⅜" (3.5cm) wide strips.

> **Hint**
>
> Cut all strips on the cross-grain of
> the fabric.

1 Arrange your fabric strips in the order you want to piece them. Sew six sets of strip sets.

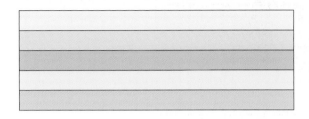

> **Hint**
>
> Be sure to sew all of the fabrics in all
> of the strip sets in the same order.

2 Press all of the seams of three strip sets up, and press all of the seams of three strip sets down. Paying careful attention to the pressing details now will make piecing the wedges easier.

3 Use the 22½° wedge ruler to cut only one strip set at a time. Place the 8¼" (21cm) line of the wedge tool directly over the top seam of the first strip set. Cut on both sides of the wedge tool.

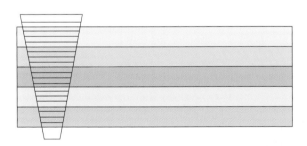

By placing the 8¼" (21cm) line over a seam, the wedges will be cut accurately.

4 Flip the ruler upside down, place the 8¼" (21cm) line directly over the bottom seam and cut another wedge.

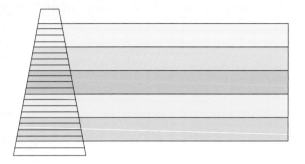

Make sure you line the left side of the ruler up to the first cut.

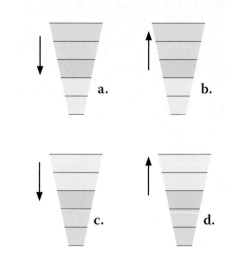

Keep these piles organized.

5 Continue to cut the remaining strip sets. Flip the ruler right side up, then upside down until the first strip set is cut. Repeat steps 3 through 5 on the remaining five strip sets.

6 Organize your wedges into four piles:

a. The first pile is comprised of eight wedges with the first color on the top edge and the seams pressed down.

b. The second pile is comprised of eight wedges with the first color on the top edge and the seams pressed up.

c. The third pile is comprised of eight wedges with the fifth color on the top edge and the seams pressed down.

d. The fourth pile is comprised of eight wedges with the fifth color on the top edge and the seams pressed up.

7 Set the third and fourth piles aside and work only on the first and second piles. Arrange the wedges in a circular pattern, alternating the wedges according to the way the seams are pressed.

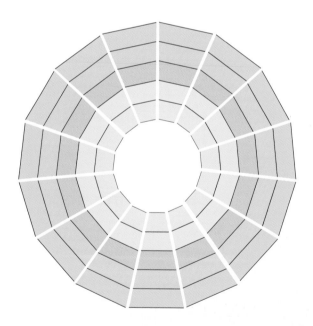

Double check to make sure that the seams are pressed in alternating directions all the way around.

8 Sew the sixteen wedges together. Do not press any seams until all the wedges have been pieced. When the wedges have been pieced into a circle, press the seams open to reduce bulk at the seams.

9 Press one of the iron-on/tear-away stabilizer sheets to the wrong side of the table topper, directly over the hole. Set the quilt top aside.

10 Fold the freezer paper in half with shiny sides together. Trace a 2¾" (7cm) diameter circle onto one side of the freezer paper using the template on page 29. Cut out two circles. Press both circles to the wrong side of the 8" (20.5cm) square of fabric for the center circles. Place the circles far enough apart on the 8" (20.5cm) square so that there is ample seam allowance around both circles. Cut out each circle, leaving at least ¼" (6mm) of fabric beyond the freezer paper for your seam allowance.

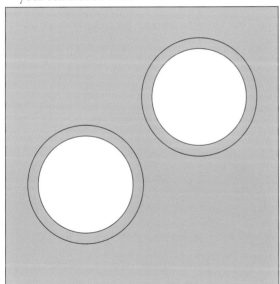

While each table topper uses only one center circle, you'll save time by completing both circles now.

11 Fold the seam allowance to the back, and hand baste the seam allowance to the freezer paper in the back of the circles. Set one circle aside for the second table topper.

The freezer paper helps you form a perfectly round circle.

12 Thread the sewing machine with the monofilament thread. Set up your sewing machine for a narrow blind-hem stitch or a narrow zigzag stitch. Center your circle to the middle of the table topper. Pin the circle to the right side of the table topper, inserting the pins into the stabilizer. Sew the circle to the table topper.

Hint

Polyester monofilament thread is better than nylon monofilament for this application because polyester does not melt as easily as nylon.

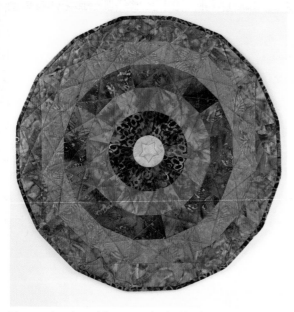

This is what the table topper looks like from the front.

13 Tear away the stabilizer from the wrong side. Remove your basting stitches from the center circle, then pull out the freezer paper. Starting at step 8, piece the second table topper.

Pin baste the top, batting and backing. The batting and backing yardage is sufficient to pin baste both table toppers at one time to large backing and batting pieces. (Refer to step 9 on page 23 to see an example of the Americana Place Mats pin basted at one time.)

I completed one of the sample table toppers using several unmarked free-motion quilting patterns. The other I quilted using continuous straight-line quilting. On the straight-line example, I started at the outside raw edge. I stitched diagonal lines through each "square," stopping to pivot at each seam intersection. I marked a star in the center circle and stitched it with contrasting thread.

After you have finished the quilting, bind each table topper.

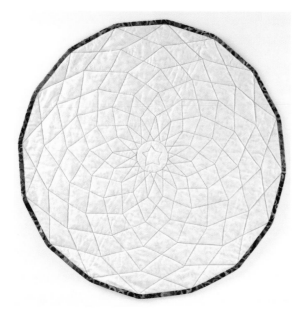

This is the straight-line quilting on the back. It is a lovely finish.

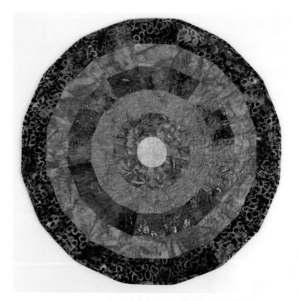

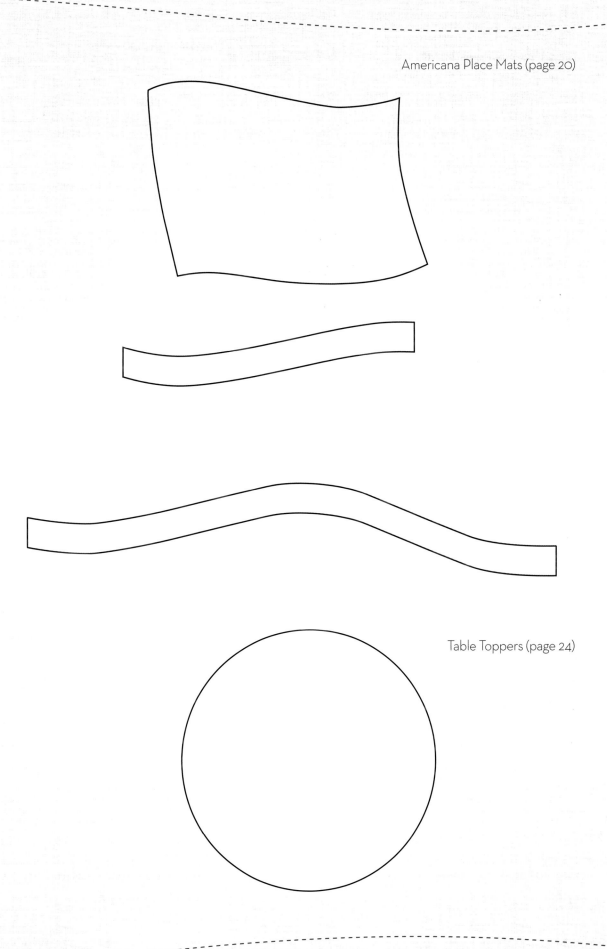

Table Toppers (page 24)

Pillow Cover

Finished size: 14" (35.5cm) square before quilting

This pillow cover will help you:

Improve either straight-line quilting or free-motion quilting.

Test quilting patterns before using them in a larger quilt. The majority of the quilting is done inside the 10" (25.5cm) center square. If you find you do not enjoy quilting a pattern inside a 10" (25.5cm) square, you won't be happy quilting it in a larger project.

Test new threads and ideas. You can quilt only the center, or you can quilt the center and border.

Practice the stitch in the ditch technique.

Materials

Sewing machine and tools

Neutral thread for piecing

Quilting thread

14" (35.5cm) pillow form

Fabric

$\frac{1}{2}$ yd. (46cm) novelty print for pillow-top border and envelope style back panels

$10\frac{1}{2}$" (26.5cm) square piece of fabric for pillow center

17" × 17" (43cm × 43cm) piece of muslin

16" × 16" (40.5cm × 40.5cm) piece of batting

Cutting Directions

From the $\frac{1}{2}$ yd. (46cm) print, cut:

One $2\frac{1}{2}$"-wide (6.5cm) strip. From this strip, cut two pieces $14\frac{1}{2}$" (37cm) long for the top and bottom borders.

One $10\frac{1}{2}$"-wide (26.5cm) strip. From this strip, cut two $10\frac{1}{2}$" × $2\frac{1}{2}$" (26.5cm × 6.5cm) strips along the grain of the fabric for the side borders.

Two $10\frac{1}{2}$" × $14\frac{1}{2}$" (26.5cm × 37cm) panels for the envelope-style pillow back.

Hint

Only the front of the pillow is quilted. The back of the pillow uses two overlapping fabric panels, known as an envelope closure. Because the panels overlap by approximately 6" (15cm), there is no need for hook-and-loop tape or zippers. The pillow form slides in and out of the envelope closure, making it easy to launder.

1 Using a $\frac{1}{4}$" (6mm) seam, sew the $2\frac{1}{2}$" × $10\frac{1}{2}$" (6.5cm × 26.5cm) strips to the sides of the pillow center. Press seams towards the border strips. Using a $\frac{1}{4}$" (6mm) seam, sew the $2\frac{1}{2}$" × $14\frac{1}{2}$" (6.5cm × 37cm) strips to the two remaining sides. Press seams to the border strips.

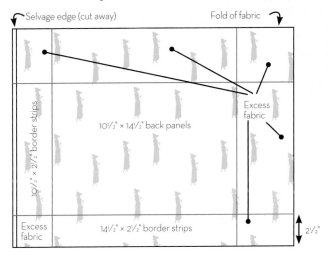

When using directional fabric, fold the fabric and cut as shown.

2 Mark the center square if the quilting pattern you wish to use requires marking.

Make sure you face all of the directional prints of the border fabric in the same direction.

In the completed sample, I added a single line of echo quilting around the outside of the stencil design after the motif was quilted.

3 Make your quilt sandwich using the 17" (43cm) muslin square for the backing. Prepare your quilt sandwich.

4 Using the stitch in the ditch straight-line machine quilting technique, stitch in the seams where the border is attached to the center square.

5 Complete the quilting using straight-line or free-motion quilting techniques.

6 Square up the completed pillow top to approximately 14½" (37cm) square, cutting away the excess batting and backing.

7 On each back panel, double fold one long edge ¼" (6mm) and sew in place. This will finish the exposed edges.

8 With right sides together, place the back panels on the pillow top, lining up the sides and overlapping the finished edges of the back panels. Place the top panel down first, then the bottom panel. Pin in place. Sew a ¼" (6mm) seam around the

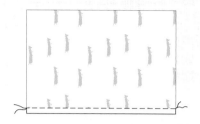

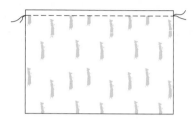

Because the example uses a directional fabric, it is necessary to complete step 7 at the top edge of one panel and the bottom edge of the other panel, as shown.

entire outside edge. Continue to pay attention to which way the panels face if using a directional novelty print.

9 In order to reduce fray, secure the outside edges with a zigzag or overlock stitch.

10 Turn the pillow inside out through the back-panel opening, and insert the 14" (35.5cm) pillow form.

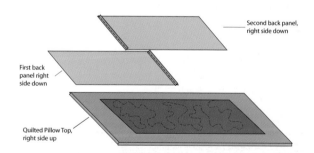

Layer the pillow-back panels as shown, pin in place and sew with a ¼" (6mm) seam.